Greek Mythology
Gods & Goddesses Explained

Fascinating stories of Greek gods, goddesses and heroes revealing the birth of ancient Greek mythology and its impact on the modern world.

By

Jeffrey Houston

Another book by Jeffrey Houston:

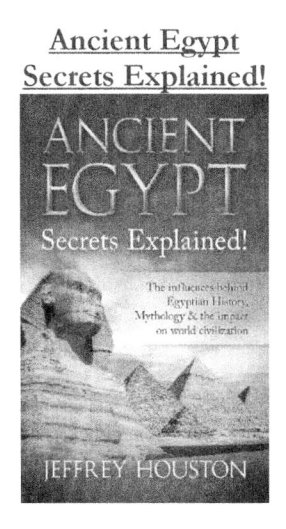

Ancient Egypt
Secrets Explained!

Copyright © 2016 by Jeffrey Houston. All Rights Reserved

This document is geared toward providing exact and reliable information in regard to the topic and issue covered. The publication is sold with the idea that the publisher is not required to render accounting, officially permitted, or otherwise, qualified services. If advice is necessary, legal or professional, a practiced individual in the profession should be ordered.

- From a Declaration of Principles which was accepted and approved equally by a committee of the American Bar Association and a Committee of Publishers and Associations.

In no way is it legal to reproduce, duplicate or transmit any part of this document in either electronic means or in printed format. Recording of this publication is strictly prohibited and any storage of this document is not allowed unless with written permission from the publisher. All rights reserved.

The information provided herein is stated to be truthful and consistent, in that any liability, in terms of inattention or otherwise, by any usage or abuse of any polices, processes, or directions contained within is the solitary and utter responsibility of the recipient reader. Under no circumstances will any legal responsibility or blame be held against the publisher for any reparation, damages, or monetary loss due to the information herein, either directly or indirectly.

Respective authors own all copyrights not held by the publisher.

The information herein is offered for informational purposes solely, and is universal as so. The presentation of the information is without contract or any guarantee assurance.

The trademarks that are used are without any consent and the publication of the trademark is without permission or backing by trademark owner. All trademarks and brands within this book are for clarifying purposes only and are owned by the owners themselves, not affiliated with this document.

Contents

Introduction 4
The Titans 7
   Cronus 7
   Hyperion 12
   Atlas 16
   Prometheus 21
The Gods 27
   Aphrodite 27
   Zeus 33
   Hera 37
   Hermes 43
   Hades 47
Conclusion 54
Thank You 57

Introduction

The Ancient Greeks are renowned for the political and technological advances they made in antiquity. Greece was the birthplace of philosophy and democracy. It was the birthplace of theater, and various "classical" architecture styles such as columns. It's where much of modern medicine made its first strides, and it's where mathematicians began to unravel the math of the universe. It's where planets got the name "planet," and where the Iliad and Odyssey were written. It's where the Olympic Games began, and it's where the Olympians resided. There are many lands that claim to be the home of the gods, but few gods are as memorable in the Western mind as the gods of the Greeks.

The Greeks existed before modern technology helped humanity understand the inner workings of the world. They hypothesized about the atom, but never physically saw it. The sun rose and the winds blew and the tides rose and fell, and none of it could be explained through the understanding of the Greeks. As such, they did what all ancient civilizations did. They created stories to explain why the world was doing what it was doing. Because these forces were so tremendous – lightning, earthquakes, and volcanoes to name a few – it was evident that whatever was controlling them was powerful. It had to be more powerful than an animal, more powerful than a man. Because these forces ravaged the planet, they were more powerful than the Earth itself. They had to be beings that transcended the Earth; they had to be gods.

There were so many natural phenomena that there had to be a plethora of gods. More importantly, they had to be described so that the Greek people would know how to please them. To upset the gods was to risk their wrath, which was both unpredictable and deadly. But describing them was tricky. The Greeks never saw them, except in their human guise, and could only assume that they behaved like humans, only more powerfully.

So the Greeks told stories, and as the decades passed, the stories became more elaborate. The result was a beautifully woven tapestry, filled with tales and allusions that people around the world are familiar with to this day. These are some of those tales:

The Titans

Cronus

Before the Olympian gods, there were the Titans. In Greek Mythology, the Titans were the first descendants of Uranus, the god of the universe, and Gaia, the goddess of the earth. They were the first class of deities that controlled the natural world, although they were the less powerful than their parents. Their powers were limited to the scope of the world; the power of Uranus was supreme over the entire cosmos. As with all things, where there is power, there is one that covets that power. As the Titans looked to their father Uranus, his youngest male child Cronus grew envious of his father's might. Cronus wanted that power for himself.

Although Cronus fostered these secret longings, he was not brazen enough to act alone, knowing he would invite the wrath of his siblings. His opportunity came in an unrelated incident. Uranus had sired several offspring on Gaia, but was not necessarily happy with all of them.

Uranus banished his children, the Cyclops and the Hecatonchires (three giants with one hundred hands) to Tartarus, a deep dungeon in the Greek underworld, and would not release them despite the repeated pleas of Gaia. As a kind, loving mother, Gaia loved all of her children, despite their horrible appearance, and grew angry with Uranus. To free her children from the evil machinations of their father, Gaia approached her other sons, the Titans, and asked them to commit one simply act. She had fashioned a sickle out of stone, and she wanted one of her sons to use it to castrate Uranus. None were bold enough to commit such an act; none save Cronus.

The youngest of the Greek Titans, Cronus was desirous to wield power like that of his heavenly father. He took the sickle and used it to castrate his father. The fact that Cronus used the sickle made sense, for Cronus commanded the harvest. As the genitals were severed from Uranus, they fell into the sea. When the droplets of blood met with the sea, they created the race of giants, they created the furies, and they created the nymphs. As his genitals fell into the sea, they gave birth to Aphrodite. Cronus' act of castrating his father symbolically broke his power over Gaia, and ended his rule, although he was still the god of the universe.

It was as a result of this action that the first gods earned the name Titans. In a tone of anger and Vengeance, Uranus had called his sons the "Straining Ones," which is "Titenes" in Greek. He threatened to get his revenge, but Cronus banished him from the earth. Before, the sky had fallen to the earth every night to lie with Gaia; now, at night, the sky remained where it was, fixed in the heavens. Cronus then placed a dragon to guard the Cyclopes and Hecatonchires in Tartarus.

Having asserted his might, Cronus became king of the Titans. As consort, he took his sister Rhea to be his queen. They ruled during an era known as the Golden Age, for during this period of time everyone lived in peace and there was no immorality. Everyone did what they were supposed to, and there was no quarrel. But the Golden Age was not meant to last; upheavals loomed in the future.

In one of those broken story chains, Uranus and Gaia approached Cronus to tell him that he would be defeated by his sons, just as he and his brothers had overthrown Uranus. At some point Gaia and Uranus must have mended fences, as well as Cronus and the father he had castrated, but that part of the story is either jumped over, or lost to history.

On hearing that he would be overthrown by his sons, Cronus made a fateful decision; as Rhea gave birth to his children, Cronus ate them. In so doing, they would not be alive to threaten him.

What followed was a tale that paralleled Cronus' own rise to power. He had been the younger son that dispatched his father with the help of his mother. His youngest son Zeus would also overthrow him with the help of his mother Rhea. His overthrow would result in the overthrow of all the Titans; they would be replaced by the Olympian Gods.

Before moving on, it is also important to discuss the other aspect of Cronus' divine status. Though he was perceived as the god of the harvest, his name had also become symbolic for the passage of time. In part, this was because the changing seasons were denoted by different stages of the harvest. Crops were planted in the spring, harvested in the summer and fall, and then the fields sat fallow in the winter, resting up to be put to use again the following season. The other reason Cronus is seen as being linked to time was his consumption of his offspring.

In a very metaphorical sense, people began to see Cronus eating the Olympians in the same way that time devours the life of a person. He was not, however, the official god of time; the Greek god of time was Chronos (please note how easy it would be to make a mistake here).

Cronus and Chronos. One a Titan and one a god. One presided over time in its most observable and necessary stages, while the other was merely there to ensure that the universal clock ticked ever forward. Despite the ambiguity, it is easy to see the effect that Cronus had over time; as the king of the Titans he had his fingers in many pies.

Though god of the harvest, the success of the Greek crops depended on other gods as well. After all, without sunlight, there would be no plants. As such, the Greeks not only revered Cronus for the harvest, but also Hyperion for the sun, the moon, and the stars.

Hyperion

Hyperion was one of the twelve Titans of ancient Greece. He stood beside his brother Cronus and assisted him as they castrated Uranus and drove him back to the sky. He clearly supported his brother, though he lacked the daringness to perform the deed himself. And perhaps it is with a closer look into Greek Mythology that the reason can be seen; when it comes to the Titans, none is as obscure as Hyperion.

To many, to make his role in Greek Mythology easier to understand, Hyperion is the god of the sun. Yet this is misleading. Hyperion had as his wife his sister Theia, and between them they had three children. The firstborn was Helios, who was the sun. Next was born Selene, who was the moon. Lastly was born Eos, who was the dawn. The offspring of Hyperion were undoubtedly important to ancient man, and in a manner of speaking Hyperion became the god of the sun, moon, and dawn. But that's the same as giving the father credit for something his child has created, for the simple reason that he bore them. It's easier to explain Hyperion this way, because the historical record doesn't leave much else.

Unlike the other Titans whose names would be remembered and catalogued as the Greeks recounted the stories of the Clash of the Titans, Hyperion does not even appear as a footnote. His lasting claim to fame is in the *Hymn to Helios,* one of several anonymous poems from ancient Greece that are slightly Homeric in style. In it, the reference to Hyperion comes when the author is addressing Theia, mentioning only that she is wife to Hyperion. In other examples, Helios is referred to as "Helios Hyperion," giving the connection to him and the sun, though in later texts he and Helios exist as separate entities.

Despite the vagueness of his position among the Titans, however, Hyperion is considered to be one of the four pillars supporting the world. He is also viewed as the god of watchfulness, wisdom, and light.

The light is obvious, for his children represent the heavenly bodies that illuminate the world. But light also represents knowledge; the reason the Dark Ages are called "dark" is because of the loss of the knowledge of classical antiquity. He is also heavenly, peering down on the world from the periphery or from the celestial vantage of his children.

Cronus may have been the king of the Titans, but he did not watch over the ancient Greeks in the same manner as Hyperion. Cronus did not have the same depth of understanding; he did not have the same wisdom.

This central theme of light and wisdom radiated around Hyperion, and caused him to be seen in a different sort of way. Uranus, the supreme god of the universe, was tangible; he was visible as the night sky. Cronus, the king of the Titans, could be seen in the harvest. But light caused you to bow instinctively, to divert your eyes from its blinding presence. Wisdom can be understood, but it can't truly be taught. It can be felt, but it can't be seen. To many, including later philosophers, Hyperion took on the nature of something called the "first principle." In philosophical terms, it's a way of describing something as the creative beginning and purposeful end of all things. It is ineffable, indescribable, and most often referred to as "the One." It's a singular entity of absolute existence; it is so simple that it cannot even be said to exist. Over the centuries, this attribute has been given to Hyperion. It is the same attribute with which Christians imbue their God.

It is an interesting and complex way to look at a simple mythological figure that barely appears in the ancient lore. His non-involvement in the feud between the Titans the Olympians served only to enhance his name, though it was not spoken once in the retelling. A proud parent, his children carry his legacy of illumination, both literally and figuratively. To the Ancient Greeks, Hyperion was the being behind the beings, all knowing and all seeing. He was a pillar that separated the earth from the heavens. He was beyond the petty bickering of both gods and men; he had existence to tend to.

Atlas

The ancient Greeks were the first civilization to hypothesize that tiny, indivisible particles made up all matter. Greek mathematicians made observations of the sunlight at noon over various areas, and were able to determine that the world was round centuries before Columbus' famed expedition. The Greeks were responsible for these and many more accomplishments, but one prevailing notion remained. To the Greeks, as well as to every other ancient society, the earth was perceived as stationary, despite its shape. The sun, the moon, and the heavens all wheeled about the earth according to the dictates of the gods. The one certainty in life was that the ground beneath their feet was solid and unshifting, and that the heavens would not crash down upon their heads.

The Greeks were secure in this belief for one reason: Atlas. During the war between the Titans and the Olympians, the Titanomachy, Atlas sided with the Titans against Zeus and his siblings. Ultimately, the Olympians would prevail over the Titans, and the Titans were punished for standing against Zeus, as well as for their misdeeds. Many were sent to the depths of Tartarus, the deepest part of the underworld, but others were put to work.

As punishment for his participation in the Titanomachy, Zeus commanded Atlas to hold the heavens aloft. This action would forever sever the heavens from the earth.

Atlas was chosen for this task because of his strength. In Greek lore, he became known as "enduring Atlas," for his task was one which never ended. If Atlas took the slightest break, the heavens would come crashing down on gods and mortals alike. It was an arduous task, and not necessarily one that Atlas reveled in; luckily for him, there was a loop-hole. Atlas would be able to release his burden if another came along and willingly took up the task of holding up the heavens. So he sat there, supporting the heavens, all the while waiting for such a person to come along.

For eons Atlas sat there waiting, until one such individual happened upon him. The man's name was Hercules, and in truth he was no man; he was a demi-god.

He was the son of Zeus. Hercules was atoning for a past sin; in a state of madness he had gone crazy and killed his wife and children. After praying to Apollo for guidance, he was told that he could atone for his crime by serving Eurystheus. Eurystheus, in turn, had Hercules perform twelve impossible labors. Atlas was number eleven.

Hercules' eleventh task was to ascend Mt. Olympus and retrieve the golden apples that were grown by Zeus. This task seemed nigh impossible; the orchard was protected by a one hundred-headed dragon named Ladon. The apples were also guarded by the Hesperides, who were nymphs as well as the daughters of Atlas. Hercules knew he couldn't brazenly walk into the orchard and get an apple. But he knew who could.

Hercules approached Atlas as he stood there with the heavens on his shoulders. He had been guided there by Prometheus, who will be discussed later. In return for a favor, Prometheus had developed a plan for Hercules to get the apples and complete his labor. Prometheus knew how much Atlas hated bearing the weight of the world upon his shoulders, and also knew that Atlas would enjoy an opportunity to shrug off such a massive weight. Hercules asked Atlas if he could walk into the garden and gather some apples while visiting his daughters. Atlas readily agreed and shifted the heavens onto the shoulders of Hercules. Hercules in turn bore the weight of the world on his shoulders while Atlas went to the orchard.

On returning, Atlas hoped to trick Hercules into accepting the responsibility of holding the heavens forever on his shoulders.

Finally the moment that Atlas had hoped for had arrived. He told Hercules that he would return the apples to Eurystheus if Hercules would continue to hold the heavens for him. Hercules could sense that there was something more behind the offer made by Atlas, so he pretended to agree. He only asked Atlas to hold the heavens one more time so that he could put some padding onto his shoulders. Atlas took the burden once more, rejoicing in his mind that he would only have to carry it for a little longer. As soon as he placed them onto his shoulders, however, Hercules stooped low and gathered the golden apples, and then ran off. Atlas, holding the heavens, could do nothing to stop him; Hercules had tricked him. And so Atlas would continue to hold the heavens.

In Greek mythology, Atlas was said to hold the heavens. Over time, however, through various artistic representations, Atlas came to be seen as the god who held the earth. This image was later reinforced as westerners began to call maps by the name of "atlas." Over time, Atlas also became synonymous with the western mountain range in North Africa, now named the Atlas Mountains. Zeus had exiled Atlas to the West, and to the Greeks the mountains looked as if they were supporting the heavens. Later legends would claim that Atlas was turned to stone by Perseus, who showed him the severed head of Medusa, thus becoming the Mountains.

To the Greeks, the role of Atlas was important, but it was also one that was easily overlooked. Aside from Poseidon's earthquakes, the earth never moved, and so for the most part they had no reason to worry. They would think of the god when talking about strength or about colossal burdens, but his role in their lives was secondary. Among the Titans, despite their fall, there was one who held a very special place in the soul of the Greeks.

Prometheus

In the days before the Olympian gods, there were many Titans. These Titans all held special powers and certain attributes. There was a hierarchy among the Titans; some of them were more powerful than others. The Original Twelve were by far the most important. Next in line came their offspring. Prometheus was one such Titan, the son of Iapetus, the god of crafting and mortality. Iapetus fought alongside his brother Cronus during the Titanomachy, and just like his brother, he was imprisoned for eternity into Tartarus. Prometheus' brother Atlas also took up the call to arms against the Olympians, and was rewarded in defeat with the punishment of holding the heavens on his shoulders. But Prometheus had abstained from the conflict; in fact, in some accounts, Prometheus had assisted Zeus in his overthrow of the Titans. Because of this, Prometheus was spared Zeus' punishment despite being a Titan, and he was welcome into the court of Zeus.

In time, Prometheus would create mankind. Because mankind was his own personal creation, Prometheus took a very special interest in man. He took it upon himself to teach man, to show them what it meant to live.

He taught them how to think, he taught them math, and he taught them science; he taught them the very nature of civilization. As a result, mankind became civilized, and they thrived in the world that the gods had created for them.

As it turned out, the world had not been created for man. Mankind was made to worship the gods, which they were happy to do. To make the gods happy was to make sure that there would be a good harvest, that there would be no floods or earthquakes. Because the gods controlled everything, their happiness was important to the humans. There was only one form of praise that mankind grew resentful of: sacrifice. The gods needed food, and the gods wanted meat. Mankind had to take the beasts that they raised and sacrifice them to the gods. Because they were gods, they wanted the best portions, leaving scraps for man.

Seeing the plight of his creation, Prometheus decided to come to the aid of man. Gathering up animals, he made a deal with Zeus in order to create a standard sacrifice so that Greeks everywhere would know what was owed to the gods. Zeus agreed, and Prometheus slaughtered the animals. He then prepared two sacrifices. In the first sacrifice, he took the best pieces of meat and wrapped them within the stomach of an ox.

He then took the pile of bones and sinew and wrapped them beneath delicious layers of fat. Zeus eyed both offerings. The first did not please him, for it did not look delicious. He looked at the second and found it very appetizing. Zeus indicated his decision, and his oath with mankind was made. Only after making the decision did Zeus discover that Prometheus had tricked him. Prometheus had saved the best parts of the meat for mankind, and offered the worst portions to the gods.

Zeus reacted in a rage, descending from Mt. Olympus and stealing fire from mankind. Fire had been the gift of the gods; without their consent, mankind lost the penultimate symbol of civilization. They could no longer cook their food; they could no longer bring light to the dark. At first they had praised Prometheus for the trick he had played, but now they cried to him, urging him to help assuage their anguish. Prometheus looked around, and realized that there was only one thing he could do. Defying the will of Zeus, Prometheus stole fire from the gods and gave mankind the gift of fire. Mankind could now wield that flickering flame without the permission of the gods.

Upon learning about what Prometheus had done, Zeus raged and stormed about Mt. Olympus. Prometheus had twice defied him, and had twice made him look foolish. As king of the gods, Zeus was supposed to appear omnipotent. Prometheus guaranteed that that could not happen, and Zeus knew that he had to make an example out of Prometheus, one of the most beloved of all the gods.

With all his might, Zeus grabbed Prometheus and dragged him to the Caucus Mountains. There, he placed Prometheus into chains which the Titan could not escape from. Next, Zeus summoned up a colossal eagle, and gave it one simple instruction. Every day, the eagle would land near Prometheus and eat his liver from his living flesh. Prometheus would experience every ounce of pain caused by this action, and would not die. Once the eagle had finished, it would leave for the day. Prometheus' liver would then grow back, and the cycle would repeat itself the next day. For his insubordination, Prometheus was made to suffer this fate for the remainder of eternity.

For thirty years Prometheus experienced the same blinding pain. Day in and day out he wailed as the bird pecked into his skin, he wept as his liver was torn from his body, and he ached as his body fixed itself. He felt disillusioned that mankind had forsaken him, leaving him chained to the mountain and not even visiting him in his exile. He had done everything, sacrificed everything, for them; now they rejoiced in the spoils and paid him no mind. For thirty years he remained there, chained and broken, wailing into the emptiness.

Until Hercules came. Hercules was nearing the end of performing his twelve labors, and he was desperately seeking information about Zeus' orchard which grew golden apples. None of the gods would tell Hercules for fear of Zeus' displeasure, and at that point Hercules decided to ask Prometheus. He was suffering Zeus' displeasure every day. It was not like he had anything to lose.

Prometheus promised to help Hercules in exchange for one favor. He asked Hercules to kill the eagle that came every day to eat his liver. Hercules killed the eagle, and then freed Prometheus from the chains that bound him. True to his word, Prometheus then thanked Hercules by giving him the information he sought.

He told Hercules that he could trick Atlas into going to the orchard and getting the fruit from his daughters. The rest has been related in the tale of Atlas earlier.

One further consequence of Prometheus' action was the creation of Pandora. In Greek mythology, she was the first woman, and she brought with her a small urn to the world. Upon meeting mankind, she opened the lid; suddenly the world was filled with evils and diseases that had never before existed. She tried to replace the lid, but it was too late. The damage had been done, and the evils that had escaped into the world began tearing it apart. People fell sick and died, disasters occurred. The period of peaceful bliss and existence had ended. The time for trial and tribulation had begun. The only tools mankind had to deal with the new problems were fire and civilization, two gifts which had been given to them by Prometheus.

The Gods

Aphrodite

To western minds, the Olympian gods are much more memorable than the Titans. There are far more tales about the Olympians than there are about the Titans; in fact, most of what is known about the Titans comes from the Titanomachy, the tale of the war between the Titans and Olympians. Westerners know that Zeus is the god of the sky, and Poseidon the god of the sea. They know that Hades is the god of the underworld, and Athena the goddess of wisdom. But for most, this topical knowledge is where it ends; most cannot tell you tales associated with these gods, nor the powerful role they played in Ancient Greece. As everyone knows, Aphrodite is the goddess of love in ancient Greek lore. Yet there is more to the goddess than meets the eye.

Unlike Zeus and most of the other Olympians, Aphrodite can trace her origins back to before the Titanomachy. For unlike the others, Aphrodite was born of Uranus and not of Cronus.

When Cronus the Titan rose up and castrated his father with the stone sickle provided by his mother, his father's genitals fell into the sea. They caused a great white, frothy wave to boil to the surface, and with that wave came Aphrodite. She emerged from the water fully formed as a woman, experiencing no childhood, and was washed to shore in the shell of a clam. And so Aphrodite came to be born, preceding Zeus who would one day rule from Mt. Olympus.

She was certainly the goddess of love and beauty. When Zeus rose to power on Mt. Olympus, he feared the effect that Aphrodite would have on the other gods. Knowing their love for her, and for her beauty, he dreaded a war between his brothers, sisters, and their children.

In order to prevent this, Zeus married Aphrodite to the god of metal work and volcanism, Hephaestus. Zeus did this because Hephaestus was a lame god, who was not very attractive. He felt that Hephaestus wouldn't represent a threat to the other gods; to Aphrodite, the match was not well suited, and she compensated by constantly having affairs with other gods.

Ares, the Greek god of war, was one of her most popular suitors. Whereas Hephaestus was considered to be a calm and even-tempered god, the legends say that Aphrodite loved Ares for his violent temper and volatile nature. Another figure she was often said to consort with was Adonis. Adonis was a figure of striking beauty, and when she first beheld him Aphrodite fell in love with him. Adonis had been the child of Smyrna, and her father Theias, the king of Syria. She conceived Adonis through trickery, and when Theias found out he wanted to kill Smyrna. But the gods intervened, saving her life by turning her into myrrh tree.

Nine months later, baby Adonis was born from the tree. Aphrodite fell in love with the young Adonis, and tried to protect him from the vengeful wrath of her father. She secreted Adonis away to the underworld, and there hid him with Persephone. Aphrodite didn't know it at the time, but she was sowing the seeds of discord between her and her sister goddess.

After taking one look at Adonis, Persephone fell in love with him as well. When Aphrodite would come to visit, Persephone would fly into a jealous rage. Aphrodite would then respond in anger. As the anger and jealousy mounted, Zeus developed a solution to the problem. For one third of the year, Adonis would spend time with Persephone. For another third of the year, Adonis would spend time with Aphrodite. Then, for the last third of the year, Adonis would spend time with whomever he wanted; he chose Aphrodite.

So great would be Aphrodite's attachment to Adonis that, after his death during a hunting accident, she begged Persephone to bring him back to life.

As the wife of Hades and the goddess of the Underworld, Persephone wanted to keep Adonis there with her. Once more, Zeus intervened, and decreed that the two goddesses take turns with Adonis, having him for six months before letting the other have him.

Aphrodite would constantly play a role in these high stake romantic interludes. One of the most notable was the incident involving the Golden Apple of Discord. It was created by Eris, who was the goddess of discord. She tossed the apple among three goddesses – Aphrodite, Athena, and Hera – and all three wanted it. As always, Zeus found himself having to make a decision to deal with seemingly irrational women. Rather than make the judgment himself, Zeus chose to allow a mortal to make the decision. That mortal was Paris.

For Paris it was an amazing offer, although it could have potentially disastrous results; gods were not individuals you wanted to upset. All goddesses offer Paris something special in return for his choice. As queen of the gods, Hera offered Paris unlimited power. As the goddess of wisdom and war, Athena offered him wisdom and fame in battle. Aphrodite, the goddess of love, offered him the most beautiful woman in the world:

Helen of Troy. She then enchanted young Paris, causing him to fall in love with Helen. Paris chose Helen, and in their wrath over not being selected, the other goddesses caused the Trojan War to begin.

We began with Aphrodite given her unique birth by Uranus, made possible by Cronus. But the powers of Aphrodite are limited in comparison to those of her brothers and sisters. She exercised power over them in the form of love and lust, but in the minds of the ancient Greeks those powers mattered little in comparison to the power over the elements, and the power over death.

Zeus

Of all the Olympic Gods, none is perhaps more recognizable than Zeus. He was the king of the gods, the ruler of the sky and the commander of weather. When he was displeased he hurled lightning bolts and stormed thunderously from atop Mt. Olympus. He was an infamous adulterer, siring several gods and demi-gods from among his mortal and immortal paramours. Within the confines of most Greek legends, Zeus would always play a prominent role. It is this Zeus that is known, but what is typically overlooked is how he rose to power and how he led the Olympians to overthrow the Titans.

After overthrowing Uranus, Cronus was told by Gaia that he would be overthrown by his children. Fearful of losing power and being cast aside like his father Uranus, Cronus made a fateful decision in order to remain in power. As each of his children was born, Cronus devoured them, knowing that if he ate them they could never rise up and usurp his authority. Terrified by his actions, and pregnant with another child, his wife Rhea asked Gaia to help her come up with a plan to save the baby. Rhea fled from Cronus, and gave birth to Zeus on the island of Crete.

She then returned to Cronus with a stone wrapped in blankets. Thinking it was his son, Cronus devoured the stone; for the moment, Zeus was safe.

There are many tales that surround what happened next. In some versions, Zeus is said to have been raised by Gaia. In other accounts, Zeus was raised by various nymphs. One account has Zeus being raised by a goat, while another has him being raised by shepherds with the promise that he would keep their flocks safe from wolves. Still others report he was raised by Melissa, a nymph and the daughter of the king of Crete. Melissa allegedly fed him milk and honey. Regardless of how it came about, all of the mythology leads to the same conclusion. Zeus was kept safe from Cronus, and grew old enough to become an adult. At that point, he could challenge his father, and rescue his siblings.

Zeus was the youngest of all his brothers and sisters, just as his father Cronus had been the youngest of the Titans. Zeus had the encouragement of his mother, Rhea, to attack his father, just as Cronus had had the support of his mother Gaia to attach his father. There were strong similarities between the two figures, just as there were strong similarities in how they wrested power from their father.

By some accounts, Zeus had Cronus drink a potion which caused him to regurgitate, first the stone and then his siblings in the reverse order they had been swallowed. Other accounts tell of how Zeus cut open the belly of Cronus, allowing the stone and his siblings to fall out. In either case, the stone is permanently set at Pytho, a sign directed at mortal men that would become known as the Stone of Omphalos. His other siblings, once out of Cronus' stomach, promptly pledged their loyalty to Zeus who had freed them. Zeus had taken the first step in fulfilling the prophecy, but Cronus was not going to be stopped simply by having the contents of his stomach purged. Zeus was in open rebellion against the Titans. Cronus called his Titans to war, and Zeus led his Olympians. In Greek mythology, the battle for control of the world was beginning.

This conflict would be called the Titanomachy, which has been previously mentioned. It ripped the world apart as the Titans struggled against the Olympians to maintain their supremacy. Zeus began by releasing the Hecatonchires and Cyclopes from Tartarus. In exchange for their freedom, the Cyclopes crafted lightning bolts for Zeus, and the Hundred-Handed giants hurled boulders against the Titans. The war raged for ten years, and ultimately resulted in an Olympian victory.

Zeus cemented his victory over the Titans by casting those who had opposed him into Tartarus. For Atlas, whose strength had been injurious to the Olympians, the punishment was crushing as Zeus ordered him to hold up the sky. Zeus then divided the world amongst himself and his three brothers. They each drew lots; Zeus was given control of the sky, Poseidon was given control of the sea, and Hades was given control of the Underworld. The remaining gods were given whatever powers their personality drew them to, and they were allowed to exercise them across the face of the world. The only check on their power would occur when Zeus, Poseidon, or Hades were asked to intervene.

As he took control of the world and made himself king of the gods, Zeus married his sister Hera. He would father many children with her, but he would also father many children with his consorts. These children would all go on to achieve their own fame and reputation, and all of their tales would involve Zeus. Some such offspring include Ares, Athena, Hercules, Achilles, and Helen of Troy. Zeus would become famous in Greek mythology for his dalliances; his wife Hera would become famous for her jealousy.

Hera

Hera was the wife of Zeus and the queen of the gods. She was the goddess of women, and of marriage. In many ways Hera's role in Greek mythology is ironic; though the goddess of women, she could not prevent them from sleeping with her husband, her husband who was constantly committing adultery despite Hera's being the goddess of marriage. Despite his infidelities, she loved her husband and stood by him, though at times his actions did wound her and consume her with anger and rage. It is this broken faith between Zeus and Hera that lead to some of her more famous appearances in the Greek mythological record.

Perhaps the most famous instance of Hera's rage against her husband's philandering is found in her animosity towards Hercules. Hercules was born as part of a tryst between Zeus and Alcmene. When Hera found out about the pregnancy, she attempted to end it. She was tricked by Almene's servant, Galanthis, who told Hera that she had already delivered the baby. When Hera found out she had been duped, she turned Galanthis into a weasel. For the moment, Hercules was safe, but Hera still wanted him dead.

Hera next attempted to kill Hercules by sending two snakes into the sleeping baby's cradle. The snakes slithered in and towards the resting babe, but Hercules awoke and grabbed both snakes by the neck, killing them and then playing with their limp bodies. Hera's attempts to kill the young child continued. At one point, Zeus tricked Hera into breastfeeding Hercules. He suckled at her breast until Hera discovered that it was Hercules. At that point, she wrenched him off. As she tugged him away there was a great gushing of milk that fell across the heavens, thus creating the Milky Way.

As Hercules grew into a man, the rivalry between the two continued. Hera intervened with Eurystheus and helped to make the labors of Hercules harder. When Hercules encountered the Learnaean Hydra, Hera attempted to break his focus by sending a crab to attack his heels. In response, when Hercules stole the cattle of Geryon he also shot Hera in the left breast with an arrow. The arrow caused her great pain, a pain which continued due to the incurable nature of the wound.

The Hera-Hercules grudge never fully resolved itself, with each figure trying to find ways to spite the other.

But there are many more stories in which Hera is much more successful in dealing with her husband's lovers and his helpers.

Echo was one such helper. Echo had been given the task of keeping Hera busy while he dallied about his consorts. Echo was simply a nymph, and she did as the king of gods commanded her, engaging Hera in conversation and keeping her occupied. When Hera discovered how she had been tricked, she placed a curse onto Echo, making Echo only able to repeat the words that were said to her. It is from this ancient myth that the modern word "echo" is derived.

Still another tale of Hera's reaction to Zeus' infidelity is related in the tale of the birth of Dionysus. Zeus snuck down one night and slept with Semele, the daughter of Cadmus who was the King of Thebes. Semele became pregnant by Zeus. When Hera found out, she came down from Mt. Olympus and disguised herself as the nurse of Semele. She convinced Semele that if Zeus truly loved her, he would appear to her in his true form, and not in the disguise of the mortal he had dressed as. Semele pressured Zeus to reveal himself to her, and after he swore an oath by Styx, he cast aside his mortal garment.

Semele saw him in all his godly visage, and the pure thunder and lightning that composed Zeus destroyed Semele. Zeus, not wanting his unborn child to perish alongside his mother, took the unborn baby Dionysus and sewed him into his thigh, where Dionysus completed his gestation.

The wrath of Hera would be so great that it crossed cultures. Zeus fell for Io, who was a mortal woman and a priestess of Hera. As they were having their affair, Hera nearly caught Zeus with Io, but Zeus was able to escape the moment of detection by turning Io into a white cow. Hera still knew that something was up, and was able to convince Zeus to give her the heifer as a present. When Hera received the cow, she placed it under the protection of Argus, who had one hundred eyes. His task was to make sure that Io and Zeus remained separated. But Zeus was the king of the gods, and he ordered Hermes to kill Argus. Hermes did this by causing all of Argus' one hundred eyes to fall asleep. Upon learning of his tragic death, Hera gathered together all of Argus' eyes and placed them onto the plumage of the peacock, thereby causing its distinctive feathered pattern. She then sent a gadfly after Io the cow, causing her constant discomfort as she wandered the earth.

Eventually Io was restored to human form by Zeus, but at this point she had made it to Egypt. There, she would later assume the form of Isis according to Ovid.

Despite her temper and her attempts to keep her husband loyal, Hera was not the only one to give into tempestuous jealousies. In one instance, Zeus took pity on a mortal king Ixion. Ixion had not paid the bride-price to his father in law when he married his daughter, and in response his father-in-law had stolen some of Ixion's horses. Ixion did not initially retaliate; instead he invited his father-in-law to dinner. When he arrived and sat down at Ixion's table, Ixion murdered him. He had broken the ancient code of guest-friendship, where anyone who was invited to dinner under your roof was also entitled to your protection. It was forbidden to kill a guest in one's home. His act of murder drove Ixion crazy, and no priest would offer him absolution for his crime.

Thus Zeus took pity on the poor mortal, inviting him to Mt. Olympus to dine with the gods. Yet while he was there, he fell in love with Hera, and became lustful towards her. Zeus found out about this, and before any action could be taken he put a stop to it. Using a cloud disguised as Hera, he lured Ixion into a trap.

He blasted Ixion with a thunderbolt and ordered Hermes to tie him to a spinning wheel consumed by fire. Ixion was then cast into the heavens, to burn and spin for eternity. Zeus may have been unfaithful to his wife, but he loved her and would not let any other man have her.

Hermes

Hermes was the messenger of the Greek gods, swiftly traveling between the realm of mortal men and ageless gods. Because of his swiftness of foot, he was the god of travelers and traders. He was known for his tricks and his deceitful nature, which was one of the reasons that he was the god of thieves. His tricky nature also caused him to be the god of oration and wit, where people were expected to be slightly loose with the truth. Hermes casually crossed the borders between mankind and the divine, and as such he was the god who spirited the souls of the departed to the underworld, taking them to Charon. He was the god of roads, and the god of sports. In short, the name of Hermes was used by nearly everyone and everything, and he was one of the deities most often prayed to by the rabble of ancient Greece.

In large part due to his mercurial nature, Hermes served many functions and played many roles in the annals of ancient Greece. Several of his tales have already been related in this text; he was ordered by Zeus to kill Argus so that Zeus could resume his adulteress relationship with Io. Hermes was then approached by Zeus to fashion an eternal wheel of spinning fire on which to place Ixion.

Hermes was a god that could get things done, and was not afraid of getting his hands dirty.

Hermes played an important role in the Trojan War as well as the tale of Odysseus returning home. Hermes sided with the Greeks in their struggle against the Trojan, but his fickle nature allowed him to protect the Trojan king Priam as he walked into the camp of the Greeks to retrieve his slain son Hector. Odysseus was the great-grand son of Hermes, and as such Odysseus possessed many of his ancestor's capacities for tricks. Hermes was prayed to as the Greeks devised the plan to leave the Trojans a gift of a wooden horse filled with Greek soldiers. The plan was successful, and the Greeks defeated the Trojans with the help of Hermes.

Hermes would re-appear in the tale as Odysseus attempted to find his way home. He warned Odysseus when Circe had turned his shipmates into animals, telling him to chew on an herb imbued with magic to prevent the same spell from affecting him. Later on his journey, Odysseus was once more waylaid, this time on the island of Calypso. After remaining there for a number of years, Zeus ordered his release, and Hermes was dispatched with the message.

When Odysseus returned home, he found his wife surrounded by suitors all trying to usurp his husbandly roles. Odysseus slew them all, and as they died Hermes was there to escort their souls to the underworld.

The tools of Hermes' trade were disguises, lies, deceit, trickery, and stealth. When Zeus created Pandora to send down to mankind and punish them with woman, these were the traits that Hermes offered up and placed inside Pandora's Box. Luck and skill were also important parts of the cult of Hermes. It was he who introduced the Greeks to games of chance like rolling dice and playing cards. But it was games of skill which became some of the hallmarks of the Greek tradition.

Hermes was said to have invented the sports of wrestling and boxing, as well as inventing various racing games. In time, these sports would be celebrated throughout Greece, and a contest among all the city-states called the Olympic Games would be held. The athletes competing in these events would offer praises and sacrifices to particular gods for certain attributes, such as strength. But most of the fleet footed racers would pray to the messenger god Hermes, known for his ethereal speed. Wrestlers and boxers would pray to Hermes, for he was cunning and strategic. He was also international.

Hermes was the god that crossed boundaries and delivered messages. He was the god of trade and travelers, and all asked for safe and bountiful journeys. Because of the role he played among travelers, the ancient Greeks would mark the extent of their territories with pillars that were decorated with a statue of Hermes.

Although he was not the king of the gods, nor was he a relatively high-ranking deity, Hermes was popular. He was well known to the people, who loved him for the things he presided over. Sports, trade, travel, and even thievery would affect the day to day life of the ancient Greeks far more than a wrathful storm caused by Zeus. To the Greeks, Hermes was the most like them. He was not feared and dreaded the way that others were.

Hades

Hades was one of the gods most feared and dreaded, for a visit from Hades signified the end of life. Hades, to the ancient Greeks, was the god of the underworld. He was one of the three primary Olympian brothers, along with Zeus and Poseidon. When he and his brothers chose lots to determine the realm over which they would rule, Hades was given supreme control over the underworld. Though perhaps not as glamorous as being god of the sky like Zeus, with all its thunder and majesty, or god of the sea like Poseidon, with all its boundless depths and bountiful fishing, the underworld would prove to be a unique domain to rule. Hades would make it very much his own.

Hades had been the first-born of the Olympian gods, and as such had been the first to be consumed by his father Cronus. When Zeus forced Cronus to regurgitate his siblings, Hades was the last out, essentially turning him into the youngest. During the battle between the Olympian Gods and Titans, Hades proved himself to be ferocious in battle and helped win the throne for his brother. Happy to serve, some ancient tales of Hades talk of his disappointment at receiving the responsibility of governing the underworld.

Once there he ruled with an iron fist, forcing all souls that arrived to abide by his rules despite what their status had been in the real world.

Afraid of incurring his wrath, the ancient Greeks refrained from speaking his name. This same trait would eventually carry over into various other cultures. In fact, many of the ancient Greek tales do not mention Hades at all, for they were fearful of drawing his attention to them. Despite this fear, Hades rarely sought to curse the living. He was not an evil or vindictive god; in fact, he was largely indifferent to the pursuits of the living. When he would make his occasional trips to the surface, Hades would wear his helmet of invisibility so as not to be observed. He would wear this helmet of invisibility on one of his most daring adventures, and one of the few stories in which Hades played a dominant role.

Hades was always surrounded by dreary death and the gloomy colors of the underworld. One day while walking the surface he stumbled across the most beautiful thing he had ever seen; a beautiful, vibrant young virgin named Persephone. She was the daughter of Zeus and of Demeter, and Hades was determined to marry her. He asked Zeus for Persephone's hand, and Zeus did not object to it.

Zeus did say that Demeter would never allow it, however, for she would not want her daughter to live in the gloom of the underworld. Between the two of them, Hades came up with a simple solution; he would abduct Persephone.

On one sunny day Persephone was out on a Sicilian plane, frolicking amid the flowers and sunshine. Suddenly, Hades came racing across the plain in his chariot drawn by four horses. He chased Persephone down and had his way with her, taking her virginity. In the aftermath of the assault, the ground was symbolically strewn with flowers of every color. He scooped her up and drove his chariot into a massive hole which had opened in the earth. Persephone cried out, but no one could hear her. As the chariot raced through the hole, it closed behind them, swallowing Persephone into the earth.

A short while later, Demeter came to the plain looking for her daughter. She called out her name but could not find Persephone anywhere. She looked everywhere, beneath every rock and every blade of grass, travelling to the ends of the earth. For nine full days she searched, frantic to find her child, growing angrier as she failed to do so. She did not eat, she did not sleep, and as her fury grew she destroyed lands and livestock, as well as anything else in her path.

Despite her exhaustive search, she could find no trace of her daughter. In her frustration and anger, she threatened to leave the world barren and destroy mankind if Persephone could not be found. As the goddess of the harvest and livestock, this was no empty threat; something had to be done.

On the tenth day, the goddess Hecate came to Demeter and told her that Persephone had been stolen, but she didn't know who had done it. In order to figure out who had abducted her daughter, Demeter and Hecate next went to Helios, the god of the sun. Perched high in the sky, Helios saw everything that happened underneath him. When asked, he replied that he had seen Hades abduct Persephone and take her to the underworld with him. He then tried to convince her that Hades was a suitable match for her, as Hades ruled one third of the universe and was the brother of Zeus. But Helios' appeals fell on deaf ears; Demeter wanted no part of the arrangement, despite the consent of Zeus.

Knowing what had happened, and the involvement of Zeus and Hades in the abduction, Hera disguised herself as a mortal woman and roamed the world. As she roamed, she caused all plants and animals to die, creating a famine that soon spread across the entire world.

Before long all of mankind was perched on the brink of annihilation. Zeus knew that he had to intervene with Demeter in order to save mankind.

At first Zeus attempted to use his prestige as king of the gods to sway Demeter. He commanded all the other gods to go to her, to beseech her to stop her course, but Demeter would not relent. She continued to kill the crops and fields of the world, and mankind continued to perish as a consequence of her wrath. It became obvious to Zeus that a parade of gods would not suffice. He would need to take direct action. He promised to resolve the issue for Demeter.

Zeus talked to his brother Hades through the messenger god Hermes, and told Hades that he would have to bring Persephone back. Persephone had grown sad while in the underworld, and had refused to eat any food. Hades loved her, but agreed to let her go as he saw the destruction she was bringing upon herself through starvation. He approached her and told her he would send her back to the surface, but asked that she first take nourishment. Persephone agreed and ate a small pomegranate seed. She didn't realize it at the time, but it was a trick; anyone who ate the food of Hades was forever bound to the underworld.

Hades had once more gained the upper hand in the struggle for Persephone.

The gods sat stunned at the defiant act of Hades, and all were perplexed at what step could be taken next. Having tasted the seed, Persephone was forever chained to the underworld. Eventually, a compromise was reached between Demeter and Hades. It had been created by Rhea, their mother, and proposed that Persephone would spend half the year with Hades and half the year with Demeter. The two reluctantly accepted. They both got what they wanted: Persephone. They both also lost what they wanted: Persephone. For the remainder of eternity, the two would play tug of war with Persephone.

This eternal struggle over Persephone would be manifested in the yearly changing of the seasons. Whenever Persephone made her yearly trip to the underworld, Demeter grew sad. As a consequence, all the earth's vegetation would shrivel and die. For mankind, this would be autumn and winter, a precarious time when food was scarce and the future uncertain. Upon Persephone's return, Demeter would liven up and all the earth would flower and bloom. Food was plentiful, and the pains of winter were forgotten in the joys of spring and summer.

Another side effect of Hades' abduction of Persephone was her elevation to the position of queen of the underworld. In time, she became as fearful a figure as Hades, her name seldom spoken by the ancient Greeks. She took to her role, becoming as stringent as Hades in relation to the rules of the underworld. In time, she became his perfect bride, and they ruled the world of the dead side by side as equals.

As the god of the underworld, a fair amount of fear and dread was directed towards Hades. But he was not only the god of the dead; Hades was also the god of wealth. The ancient Greeks were skilled miners and smiths, and they knew that the ore and minerals they worked with came from the ground. Hades was a subterranean god, and as such the vast mineral deposits of the earth were seen as being in his keeping. As much as the ancient Greeks may have wished to avoid Hades, their path to wealth flowed through him.

Conclusion

This work has served to highlight just a sampling of the various Greek myths that have been passed down through the centuries. Ancient Greeks attempted to explain their world and their surroundings through these tales. The gods they conjured were endowed with unearthly powers, yet they remained human in appearance and characteristics. They helped the ancient Greeks establish a moral code and a barometer to measure right and wrong within society. The Greeks were one of the first civilizations whose culture was well documented and passed down through the ages; as such, Greek mythology would heavily influence western history.

Greek mythology played a profound role in the development of Roman mythology. Most Greek gods found new homes in Rome, albeit with a different name. These gods would provide the bedrock for Roman culture in the same way that they did for the Greeks. The names of the planets in the solar system would in turn be named after these Roman gods, although the Greeks were the first to coin the term "planet," meaning wanderer.

Overtime the Romans moved away from their polytheistic society, embracing the new religion of Christianity that had developed in the Middle East. Christianity called for one god, and the face that was conjured and chiseled by the Romans was the face of Jupiter, who in turn had been Zeus in Greek mythology. As the Romans struggled to turn a polytheistic society into a monotheistic one, they kept many polytheistic elements intact. The Catholic Church had saints, all of whom could be prayed to in order to intercede on the behalf of the penitent. Certain saints were prayed to for certain reasons, such as St. Christopher, the patron saint of travelers. St. Christopher had become the Roman Catholic Church's version of Mercury, who was the Roman version of Hermes.

Greek Mythology not only had a profound impact on Western religious doctrine, but the tales provided were allegorical. They could be applied to countless situations, and are still alluded to today. When people talk about a job that seems ceaseless, they call it a Sisyphean task, alluding to a king who was forced to roll a stone uphill, only to have it fall back down, the task beginning again. Another such instance is the term "narcissist," used to describe someone who is incredibly absorbed with themselves. The term comes from the tale of an ancient hunter who was very beautiful.

He would turn away those who loved him, for they were unworthy of his attentions. One fateful day he looked into a pool of water, and on seeing his reflection, fell in love with himself. He could not move from the pool of water, and there died as he gazed upon himself.

    These terms, and many like them, have all stemmed from Greek mythology. We use them in our daily vernacular; oftentimes not even understanding why we use them. We use these terms and allusions to help explain the world around us, in very much the same way that the ancient Greeks used these stories to explain the things they encountered. The tradition of storytelling to explain the often unexplainable is one of the most lasting legacies of the Greeks. The better the story, the more lasting the impression it created. Through their mythology, the Greeks created stories that were so memorable that they became just as immortal as the gods they spoke of.

Thank You

Thank you for purchasing this book, I hope you enjoyed these wonderful mythical stories and now understand who the prominent Greek gods and goddesses were and the purpose that they served for the ancient Greeks.

Why not expand your knowledge and learn about Ancient Egypt, its history and mythology. To begin your journey into ancient Egypt get Ancient Egypt Secrets Explained!

Ancient Egypt Secrets Explained!

Printed in Great Britain
by Amazon